MICHAEL ALEXANDER STRAUSS
METATECHNICAL EXERCISES I

SEE SAW SWING

FOR THE CELLO

Develop tone, technique, note reading, rhythm and intonation

Copyright 2012 by Michael Alexander Strauss

If I can stop one Heart from breaking
I shall not live in vain
If I can ease one Life the Aching
Or cool one Pain

Or help one fainting Robin
Unto his Nest again
I shall not live in Vain.

Emily Dickinson

Thank you to my teachers:

Joseph Primavera
Alice Lindsay
Thomas Lindsay
Lucy Parker
Al Filosa
Eugene Lehner
Paul Doktor
George Neikrug
Dorothee Metlitzkee
Raphael Hillyer
Scott Nickrenz
Heidi Castleman
Benjamin Zander
Karen Tuttle
Marjorie Barstow

Cover design and artwork by
Maggie.Grundy@gmail.com

See   saw   see   saw   will   you   be   my   friend?

HOW TO USE SEE SAW SWING

These exercises are an experiment designed to accelerate learning for beginning and remedial students, with positive results in improving tone, technique, shifting, double stops, ensemble playing, and rhythm.

See Saw Swing is based on Whole Brain Learning. Every line swings the student from the left hemisphere of the brain to the right as they alternate string crossings with fingered patterns. This alternation from side to side strengthens the Corpus Callosum- the nerve network that divides and connects the hemispheres- leading to progress that students describe as being "magical."

Scientifically, to reproduce the results of an experiment, it is necessary to replicate as much as possible every aspect of the experiment. Obviously, because all teachers are unique, this is impossible. However, it is possible to use *See Saw Swing* exercises as I have learned to use them: when I wrote this book, in 2006, I had no idea what I had created and didn't know how to use it. But after fourteen years of practice, combined with research on brain activity, I now have an algorithm that every teacher is free to employ.

With young students, sing the tune with the prescribed words. Always show them how to differentiate between long strokes and short strokes, and to practice the exercises in different parts of the bow. Also be certain to teach that each string has a different weight, and every time you shorten a string by stopping it, it weighs less.

See Saw Swing is built on the principle of repetition, with two notes changing in every line ("Musical Phonics"). Also, the various finger patterns and rhythmic applications are geared to mastering different pieces of music. Because it is easy for the student to learn to play the first pages, it is crucial to have them practice at least two pages at a time; the goal is to physically condition the student to play the instrument.

See   saw   see   saw   yes   I'll   be   your   friend!

WHOLE BRAIN LEARNING

To paraphrase a direction from a popular beginning violin book:
*Learn to play by perfecting one skill at a time. Do not go onto the next step until
you have command over this one.*

It sounds so simple, and seems so correct, but is that how any child learned to walk,
talk, socialize, read, or hit a baseball? Did you master one phoneme at a time, never
going on to the next sound until you had command over this one?

I don't think so.

And yet it sounds so correct to practice one step at a time, and here is why: **This is
precisely how the left hemisphere of the brain processes data.**

There is a time and place for the perfectionism practiced by the left hemisphere but not
at the beginning stages of violin study and especially not for children.

The first five lines of See Saw Swing includes all the notes of a major scale, three rhythmic
values, and many string crossings. I have had students work through the first 20 pages of
See Saw Swings in less than three months and then be promoted out of their beginner
string class in school (4th grade) to join the 5th grade orchestra, laughing all the way because
it was easy!

How? By activating whole brain learning. *See Saw Swing* students find their way around
their instruments the same way that they learned to walk, talk, count, and read: a joyfully
childish blend of exploration without fear of failing.

When they get both hemispheres of their brain in the room at the same time, they become
so much smarter!

***See Saw Swing* does this by oscillating students' attention-processing from one
hemisphere to the other, generating an accelerated learning curve. In my teaching, these
exercises bypass students' debilitating habits and effect dynamic changes at the
neuroplastic level. Whole brain learning also lights up childrens' forebrains, freeing
them to apply critical thinking to their elementary learning challenges.**

So, as your embark on your personal experiments with *See Saw Swing,* please think like a
scientist and take the challenge of replicating my experimental results.

Michael Alexander Strauss
January 29, 2020

See   saw   see   saw

THE ALGORITHM

1. ASAP have the student practice at least two pages nonstop (within four weeks).

2. ASAP practice G Major and C major sections.

3. In the first month, train student to play fingered measures vertically. One note changes per line. This is "Musical Phonics." (PARADIGM SHIFT).

4. Play the exercises in canon with your student within the first eight weeks.

5. The sooner you introduce Eb, Ab & Db major, the easier your student will make the adjustment. *See Saw Swing* is a paradigm shift in violin training that operates on the principle of immersion.

7. Within eight weeks of lessons, combined with musical pieces, the student can feel comfortable alternating D Major and Eb Major. At this point, pencil in natural signs in D Major (etc.) to turn the D Major scale into a Mixolydian scale (Low 2nd on the A,but high second on the D string); this conditions the student to easily negotiate the low second fingers of Bach Minuets (8-12 weeks).

8. As soon as the student is comfortable switching between D Major and Eb Major, take them to E Major and the 1st finger bridge. This trains the high 3rd finger (10-14 weeks).

9. Pencil in slurs within the first 8 weeks of study. The longer you wait to teach slurring, the more difficult it becomes to learn (PARADIGM SHIFT).

10. Introduce the rhythm pages within the first eight weeks. Not only should you have them apply the rhythms to the exercises, but practice the rhythm pages in canon, which creates a steady quarter note beat (PARADIGM SHIFT).

11. At this point, your student is ready to skip to the final chapter, Vocalization, and learn the See Saw melody in ascending half steps. The earlier you start your beginner on shifting, the more easily and freely the child will take to it (PARADIGM SHIFT!).

12. The hooked bowing exercises prove to be difficult for most students. Differentiate the long stroke (arm) from the short stroke (wrist).

13 The double string crossing section is an advanced exercise.

14. Within three months, students should be practicing eight pages per day nonstop and accelerating the tempo. Always alternate exercise practice with perfecting their new music.

15. Practice in canon frequently to improve listening, rhythm and ensemble skills..

16. TheVocalization exercises, which use all the fingers, are crucial for ear training. You will find that mastery of half step shifts -which mimic a voice student's vocalization exercises- make it easy for the student to shift from first to third position (PARADIGM SHIFT!).

17. The E Major page near the end of the book introduces shifting between different positions. Once your students feel comfortable, have them go back to the beginning of the book and practice *See Saw Swing* exercises in different positions.

18. Within the first six months, have your students practice the final page, Double Stops. Then, apply double stop practice to every exercise.

19. When your students are able to negotiate every exercise in this book, even if they are still learning music at the level of Suzuki Volume 2, they will be ready to learn anything at the level of Suzuki Volume 4. I have had remedial students make the leap after three months of lessons. Beginners aged 9 and over can attain this in six months (PARADIGM SHIFT!!!).

SEE SAW SWING

Michael Strauss

Be sure to use long strokes for the quarter notes, and very short, for the eighths.

When crossing strings, take time to rotate your shoulder and change arm level.

8

10

159

163

167

171

175

179

183

187

191

195

12

14

LOW 1ST FINGER

Here we introduce the low 1st finger.

There is now a large space (major 3rd) between the 1st & 4th fingers.

And this is a low 2nd finger, exactly halfway between the first and fourth.

61

65

69

73

77

81

85

90

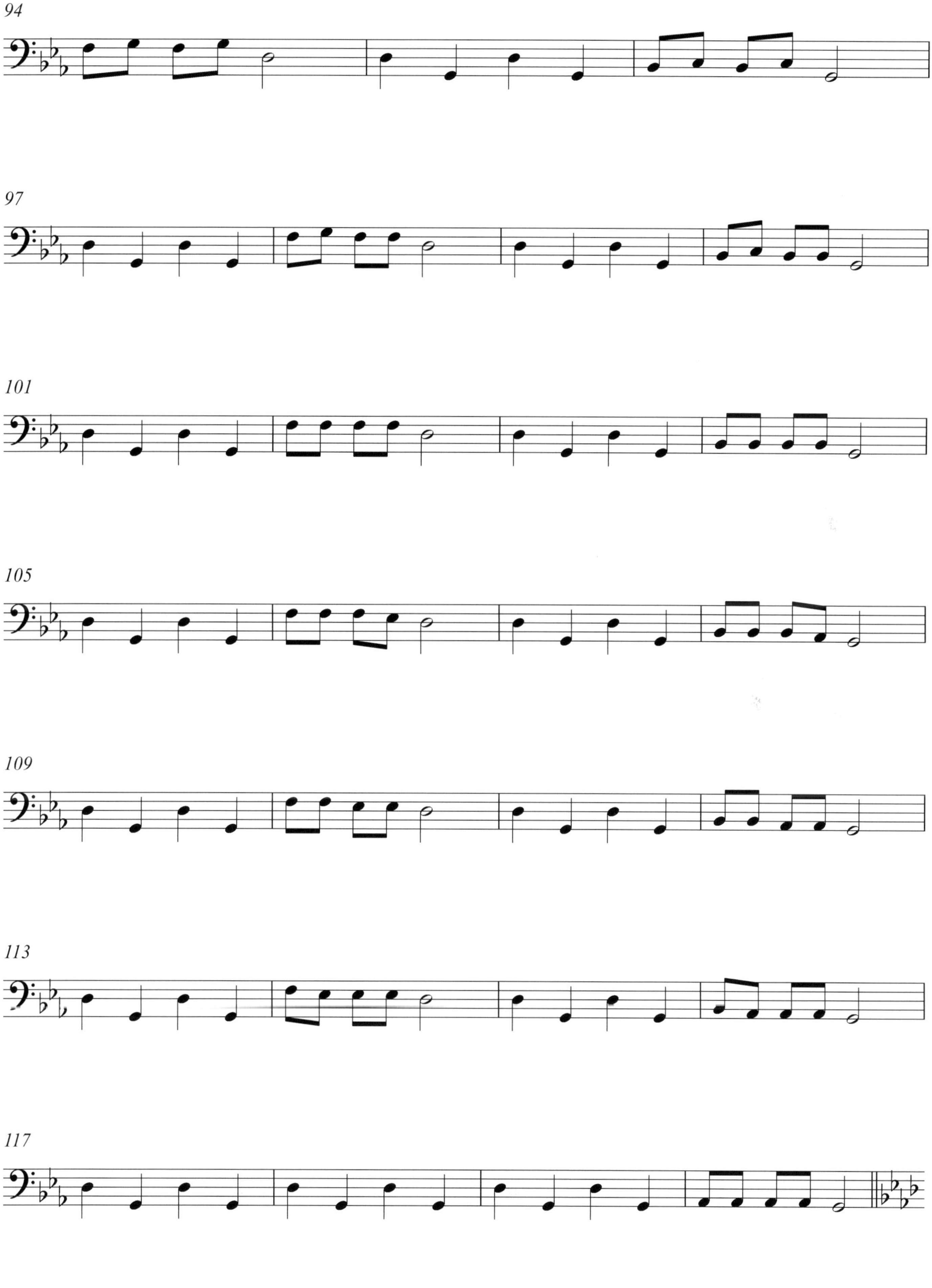
94
97
101
105
109
113
117

22

FIRST FINGER BRIDGE

Keep first finger down across both strings.

24

261

265

269

273

277

281

Keep first finger down across both strings.

313

317

321

325

329

333

337

341

345

349

353

357

361

365

28

Keep first finger down across both strings.

30

HOOKED BOWS, RHYTHMS, LOW FIRST FINGER BRIDGE

Keep the first finger
down across both strings.

Long stroke, short stroke;
long stroke, short stroke.

Two short; three long.

Tricky rhythm in half position.

89

Keep the first finger
down across both strings.

93

97

101

105

109

113

149

153

158

162

165

169

173

177

181

185

189

193

197

201

205

209

213

217

221

225

229

TRIPLETS

If you use whole bows, the triplets will alternate frog and tip; be sure tip and frog sound identical.

29

33

37

41

45

49

53

57

61

65

69

73

77

81

42

DOUBLE STRING CROSSINGS/EIGHTH NOTE CROSSINGS

Use the whole arm and some wrist for double string crossings. Use only the wrist for single crossings.

Keep both fingers down when crossing strings.

57

61

65

69

73

77

81

85

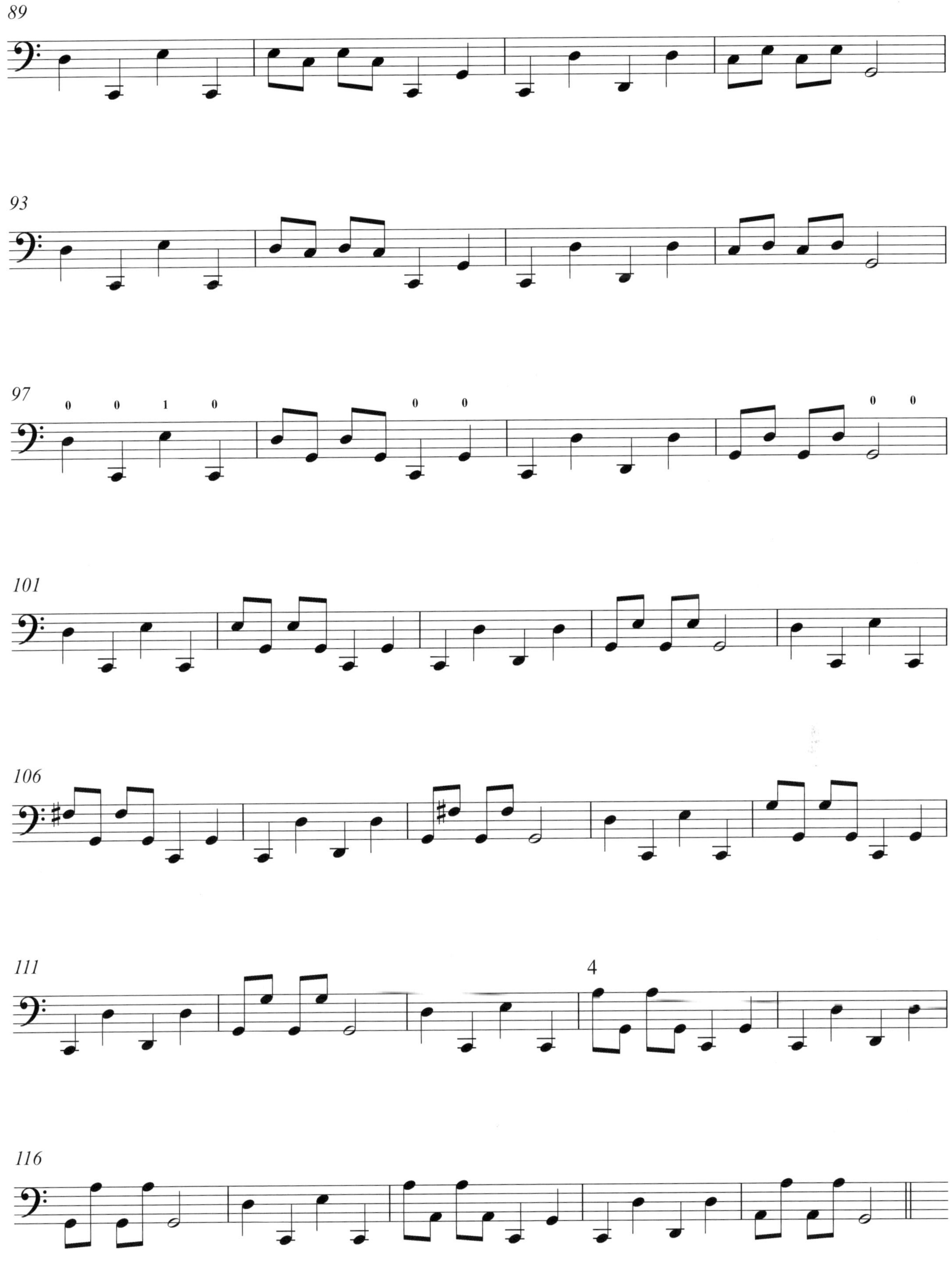
89
93
97
0 0 1 0
0 0
0 0
101
106
111
4
116

INTRODUCTION TO SHIFTING AND POSITIONS

In this introduction to positions, maintain a whole step between 1st & 3rd fingers.

As you shorten the string, put your two fingers closer together, ever so slightly, to stay in tune.

Use your ear and play as if you were singing. Be sure to lighten the bead as you climb.

Now, reverse the string crossing and play the quick notes on the lower string.

As you climb your strings, the spacing between fingers decreases symmetrically.

By now, you get the idea; always slide your whole hand up a half step.

II

Be certain to read the music as you play, to train yourself to play in these different positions.

Now we add all the fingers.

This sameness keeps it symmetrical and makes it easier to learn.

The intervals always stay the same.

50

This sameness keeps it symmetrical and makes it easier to learn.

The intervals always stay the same.

211

216

221

226

231

236

Made in the USA
Columbia, SC
25 February 2020